Th

MW01179131

Wishes

by Mark Simons
illustrated by Tracie Grimwood

SCHOOL PUBLISHERS

Printed in the United States of America

ISBN 10: 0-15-351285-7
ISBN 13: 978-0-15-351285-8

Ordering Options
ISBN 10: 0-15-351211-3 (Grade 1 Advanced Collection)
ISBN 13: 978-0-15-351211-7 (Grade 1 Advanced Collection)
ISBN 10: 0-15-358025-9 (package of 5)
ISBN 13: 978-0-15-358025-3 (package of 5)

3 4 5 6 7 8 9 10   179   15 14 13 12 11 10 09 08

One day, Tom saw a man in the forest.

"Can I have some food?" the man asked.

"You can have this plum," Tom said.

It was all the food Tom had.

"You were very good to me," said the man. "You can have three wishes."
This made Tom happy, and he ran all the way home to tell Tess.

"I wish for a lump of gold so that we can get some food," said Tom.
Flash! Tom had a lump of gold.

"You could have wished
for a big bag of gold!"
Tess said.
"I wish you were not here!"
Tom said.

Flash! Tess was not there.
"Tess?" Tom called.
Tom was upset.

"I wish Tess were back!"
he said.
Flash! Tess came back.
Tom was very happy.
"Now let's get some food!"
said Tom.

That night, they asked the man with the wishes to come for a yummy ham dinner.